THE ATTRIBUTES OF GOD

for KIDS

Lydia White

Copyright © 2017 Lydia White.

All rights reserved. No part of this book may be used or reproduced by any means, graphic, electronic, or mechanical, including photocopying, recording, taping or by any information storage retrieval system without the written permission of the author except in the case of brief quotations embodied in critical articles and reviews.

Interior Art Credit: Taylor Nelson   www.vosseco.com
Editor: Tamara Robinson   www.integrityediting.net

All Scripture quotations, unless otherwise indicated, are taken from the Holy Bible, New International Version®, NIV®. Copyright © 1973, 1978, 1984, 2011 by Biblica, Inc.™ Used by permission of Zondervan. All rights reserved worldwide. www.zondervan.com The "NIV" and "New International Version" are trademarks registered in the United States Patent and Trademark Office by Biblica, Inc.™

Scripture taken from the New King James Version®. Copyright © 1982 by Thomas Nelson. Used by permission. All rights reserved.

Scripture quotations are taken from the Holy Bible, New Living Translation, copyright ©1996, 2004, 2007, 2013, 2015 by Tyndale House Foundation. Used by permission of Tyndale House Publishers, Inc., Carol Stream, Illinois 60188. All rights reserved.

The Holy Bible, English Standard Version® (ESV®)
Copyright © 2001 by Crossway, a publishing ministry of Good News Publishers.
All rights reserved.
ESV Text Edition: 2016

This book is a work of non-fiction. Because of the dynamic nature of the Internet, any web addresses or links contained in this book may have changed since publication and may no longer be valid.

ISBN-13: 978-1976208119
ISBN-10: 1976208114

For Courtney & Caleb

We continually ask God to fill you with the knowledge of His will through all the wisdom and understanding that the Spirit gives, so that you may live a life worthy of the Lord and please Him in every way: bearing fruit in every good work, growing in the knowledge of God, being strengthened with all power according to His glorious might so that you may have great endurance and patience, and giving joyful thanks to the Father, who has qualified you to share in the inheritance of His holy people in the kingdom of light.
Colossians 1:9-12

Thank You

Thank you to my ever-supportive husband Kyle for encouraging me throughout this process and taking the lead on kid care when I was in "mad scientist" mode.

Thank you to my parents, Michael and Heather Windheuser, for rooting me in the truth of the gospel and continually reminding me that "there's a verse about that" . . . [insert teenage eye roll but adult appreciation].

Thank you to the staff of the University of Kansas Navigators, including previous directors Matt and Kori Podszus, for walking side by side with me (and Kyle) for the sake of the gospel. You lived out the truth of God's character on a campus swirling with ideas and confusion.

Thank you to Karen Vogler for speaking on the attributes of God at a Navigators women's retreat. At a time when I was questioning whether knowing God was possible, your talk led to a summer study of A.W. Tozer's *Knowledge of the Holy*, which brought my heart back to God. Your handout about God's attributes now has worn edges but is one of the resources essential to this book. My appreciation is more than I can express.

Thank you to the Mill Creek Community church family for their encouragement and support: Jeremy Krause, Cindy Hennen, Michele Welch, Tamara Robinson, and Craig Stout. Thank you to my many friends who reviewed this book and provided feedback. Thank you to Taylor Nelson for saying yes to a Bible study and yes to creating the beautiful illustrations in this book.

I am thankful to God for rescuing the low points in my life by bringing me back to His character. I am thankful that He allows me to participate in teaching my children these important truths. My prayer is that many parents and children sit together, read this book, and savor the attributes of God.

Lydia White

Preface

Although this book is intended for children, even adults can benefit from simple, concise explanations of complex topics such as the character of God. In *The Knowledge of the Holy*, A.W. Tozer writes, "What comes into our minds when we think about God is the most important thing about us."[1] As a mom of two young kids, I went looking for a children's devotional describing the attributes of God. Having been strongly influenced by Tozer's book in my own life, I wanted something similar on a much simpler level. While this devotional can never do justice to the true wonder of God's character, my hope is that it encourages adults and children to know God better.

Our society teaches our children that happiness is found by creating and expressing their self-determined identity. As Christians, we want our children to know that their identity is not self-determined but God-determined and that their life is not about self-expression but God-expression. By giving our children an understanding of the character of God, we pray that they come to love Him, love what is good, and transform their lives accordingly. We want their knowledge of God to "begin in wisdom and end in wonder."[2]

My prayer is that this book deepens our children's understanding of who God is so that their identities are rooted firmly in His identity, and that, secure in that identity, they reflect the image of God to a world that so desperately needs to see Him.

Lydia White

Resources:
1 *The Knowledge of the Holy*, A.W. Tozer, Harper San Francisco
2 *The Liberal Arts Tradition*, Kevin Clark & Ravi Scott Jain, Classical Academic Press

Other Recommended Reading:
Knowing God, J.I. Packer, InterVarsity Press
Spiritual Parenting, Michelle Anthony, David C Cook
Teaching from Rest, Sarah Mackenzie, Classical Academic Press
The Practice of Godliness, Jerry Bridges, NavPress
The New City Catechism, Crossway Publishing

Table of Contents

Parent's Guide 2
Intro: God is Real, Knowable, & Personal 4
Section 1: God's Unique Attributes 6

Unchanging 8
Infinite 10
Creator 12
Eternal 14
Self-Sufficient 16
Omniscient 18
Omnipotent 20
Omnipresent 22
Sovereign 24
Trinity 26

Let's Review 28
Quiz Time! 30

Section 2: God's Moral Attributes 32

Good 34
Just 36
Righteous 38
Merciful 40
Gracious 42
Loving 44
Holy 46
Jealous 48
Wise 50
Truthful 52
Faithful 54

Let's Review 56
Quiz Time! 58

Parent's Guide

This book is a daily devotional for parents to read with their school-age children. Following an introduction, the book is divided into ten incommunicable (unique) attributes of God and twelve communicable (moral) attributes of God.

Engage
Each chapter focuses on a single attribute with a concise definition. Readings are simple and short for young minds. They include fun questions, colorful illustrations, and a few low-prep activities to engage children as they learn each attribute.

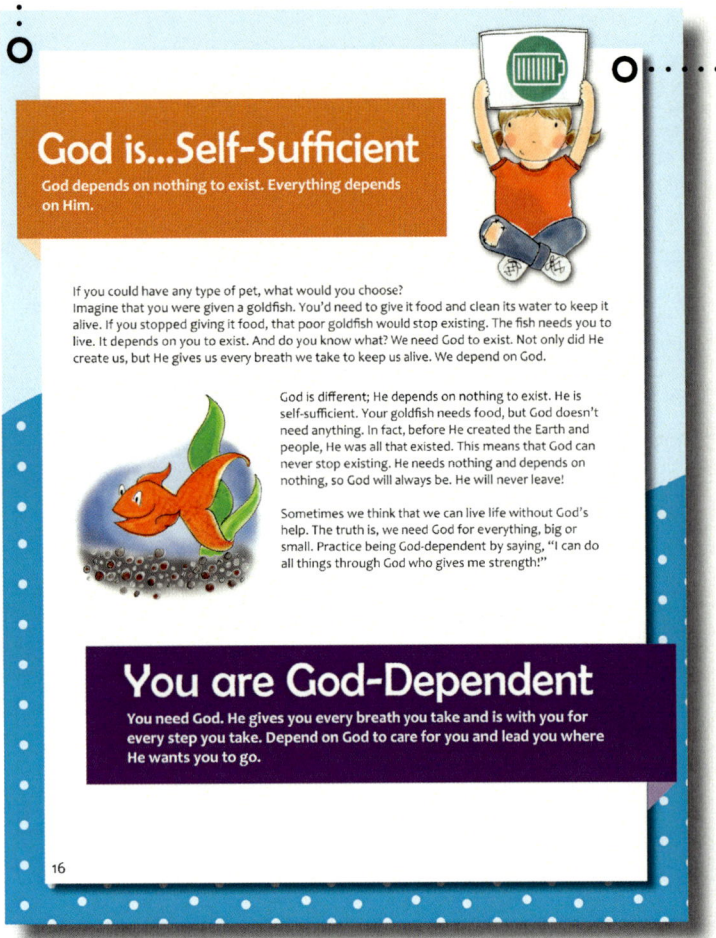

Remember
A memory icon is shown for each attribute and used on the review pages at the end of each section.

Younger Children - Say the name of each attribute by using the memory icons on the Quiz Time page.

Older Children - Learn the attribute, definition, and memory verse summarized on the Let's Review page.

Apply
Consider not only who God is, but how His character impacts our identity. As situations arise in life, remind your children who God has made them to be.

Worship
Lay the foundation for your child's personal walk with God. Spend time as a family reading God's Word and talking to Him in prayer.

Reinforce
● Look for examples of God's attributes in action by reading suggested chapters of *The Jesus Storybook Bible* or the recommended Bible passage. Consider spending two days on each attribute by alternating between *The Attributes of God for Kids* and the correlating Bible passage.
http://www.sallylloyd-jones.com/books/jesus-storybook-bible/

● Listen to songs praising God to keep God's attributes in your mind throughout the day.

Seeds Family Worship songs available online.
https://www.seedsfamilyworship.com/store/music/

INTRODUCTION

When I say "God," what comes into your mind?

Maybe you think God is "who they talk about in church" or "who we pray to at bedtime." You may think of names like "shepherd" and "father" or words like "big" and "important." You may not know anything about God and that's ok.

We'll learn more about God together!

God Is...

REAL

God is not made-up. He really exists!

Do you like to imagine? Imagine a silly made-up monster. Does your silly monster have one eye or five eyes? Is your monster purple or rainbow colored? What does your monster like to eat for breakfast: pancakes or shoelaces? Ewww! It's fun to pretend and imagine something that isn't real.

Now let's describe someone that is real. Describe the person reading this book to you. Do they have blue eyes or green eyes? Is their hair brown or blonde? Do they like to eat pickles or do they prefer strawberries?

God is not imaginary like your silly monster; He's as real as the person reading this book to you. Once you get to know Him, you'll be able to describe what He is like, His attributes. You will know what is true about God.

Isaiah 46:9b
I am God, and there is no other; I am God, and there is none like me.

KNOWABLE

We can know God through His letter to us, the Bible.

How do we find out what is true about God? We meet Him through the Bible. The Bible is God's word to us in stories, history, poems, and letters that tell us who He is and what He is like. God has also given us this beautiful world to discover His creativity, our experiences and families to understand His relationship with us, and our minds to learn about God through the Bible.

Can we know <u>everything</u> about God? NO! Because God is so big and amazing, our small human minds can't understand everything about Him. But God has given us <u>everything that we need</u> to get to know Him through the Bible.

2 Timothy 3:15
From childhood you have known the Holy Scriptures, which are able to make you wise for salvation through faith which is in Christ Jesus. (NKJV)

2 Peter 1:3
By His divine power, God has given us everything we need for living a godly life. We have received all of this by coming to know Him, the one who called us to Himself. (NLT)

PERSONAL

God is not far away. He knows you, loves you, and is always with you!

God is not a distant, far-off god who set the world in motion and left. He is not an uncaring king who doesn't know the names of His people. God is personally involved in the details of your life. He knows your name, your likes, and your dislikes. He is always there for you, and He wants to be your closest friend. The all-powerful, self-sufficient God doesn't <u>need</u> you, but He <u>wants</u> you. He wants to be close to you and pour His love into you like a good father.

James 4:8a Come near to God, and He will come near to you.

Matthew 10:30 But even the hairs of your head are all numbered.

Section 1

God's UNIQUE Attributes

What are attributes?
Attributes are characteristics that describe what we are like.

People have different types of attributes:
- **Physical:** tall or short, brown hair or blonde hair, fast or slow runner
- **Personality:** outgoing or quiet, serious or funny, creative or orderly
- **Character:** honest or dishonest, kind or unkind, thoughtful or self-centered

What are some of your attributes?

You were born with many of your attributes and others you learn as you grow. You can't change your eye color, but you can learn to be kind to others. God's attributes don't change; what was true of God when He created the world is still true of God today.

What does unique mean?
Does everyone in your family like ice cream? Yum! If you are the only one in your family who likes strawberry ice cream then you are unique, or different. Can you think of ways that you are different from the person reading this book with you?

God has many attributes that are unique, or different, from us. Let's learn about them together!

Romans 1:20
Since the creation of the world, God's invisible attributes… have been clearly seen…from what has been made, so that people are without excuse.

Jeremiah 10:6
No one is like you Lord, you are great and your name is mighty in power.

trinity

unchanging

infinite

sovereign

Unique Attributes

creator

omnipresent

omnipotent

omniscient

self-sufficient

eternal

An attribute of God is whatever God has in any way revealed as being true of Himself.
- A.W. Tozer

God is...Unchanging

God does not change. He stays the same yesterday, today, and forever!

Have you ever gotten better at something that used to be hard, like sharing with your brother or sister? Perhaps you used to cry when you had to share. As you've grown, you've learned that taking turns is loving and kind.

It's fun to get better at things that used to be hard, like tying your shoe. For us humans, change can be good, but God is different than we are. He doesn't need to get better because He is already the best. He cannot get better at loving because He never changes. He defines what perfect love is.

Have you ever changed your mind? Maybe pink was your favorite color yesterday, but today your favorite color is red (and yellow and sometimes pink). Sometimes it is ok to change your mind, but if someone changes their mind often it can be frustrating. Imagine that yesterday your teacher said to raise your hand to talk, and then today she says to shout out the answer, and then tomorrow she says to not talk at all. You would never know what you were supposed to do: raise your hand, shout, or be quiet. You would be confused and want your teacher to stop changing her mind!

God is not confusing. He doesn't change His mind, so you always know what He is like and what He wants you to do. He stays the same yesterday, today, and forever. Even if you or people in your life change their minds, remember that God doesn't change and neither do His plans for you.

You are Secure

God's truths and promises won't change. God's love for you will never leave, and His forgiveness won't be taken back. You do not need to worry about changes in your life because God holds you secure - always.

Spending Time With God

 # Listening to God

Malachi 3:6a I the LORD do not change.

Memory Verse:
Hebrews 13:8 Jesus Christ is the same yesterday and today and forever.

For Further Reading:
The Jesus Storybook Bible - "Get Ready!" pg. 170
Nehemiah 9:6-33; Hebrews 6:13-18

 # Talking with God

Unchanging God,

Thank you that you are the same God today that you were before I was born. Thank you that you do not change your mind. We can always know who you are and what you want of us. When changes happen in my life, please help me to remember that you never change. Amen

 # Praising God

God is Unchanging - Hebrews 13:8
vol 7 The Character of God by Seeds Family Worship

God is...Infinite

God is not limited by anything, and His attributes are greater than we can understand.

How many hours are in a day? That's right, there are 24 hours in one day. Half of those hours you spend sleeping, and the other half you spend awake. If you really wanted to, you could stay up all night. You could play for 24 whole hours, but the next day you might fall asleep into your bowl of cereal! Your body is limited by needing sleep.

How much do you know about outer space? You might know the names of the planets (Mercury, Venus, Earth, Mars, Jupiter, Saturn, Uranus, Neptune), but do you know the names of every star? Of course not because there are billions of stars! Your mind is limited in what it can know.

We are limited by so many things: we need to sleep, we need to eat, we can only be in one place at a time, we can only know so much.

God is is not limited like we are. He is infinite, or unlimited. God does not have a body that needs sleep or a mind that is limited in what it can know. God is outside of our physical world and is not limited by the laws of nature. He doesn't get tired or hungry. He can be many places at once, and He knows all there is to know. His love is greater than our experience of love. His thoughts are beyond what our minds can understand.

We like to think that we can do anything we want, but our limitations remind us that we are not God. Only the perfectly good God can do anything He wants. And do you know what the unlimited God wants more than anything? He wants you to rest in His unlimited love!

You are Loved Without Limits

God gives you limitations to remind you that you are not God. When you feel small, remember that your big God loves you without limits.

Spending Time With God

 ## Listening to God

Isaiah 55:8-9 For my thoughts are not your thoughts, neither are your ways my ways, declares the LORD. As the heavens are higher than the earth, so are my ways higher than your ways and my thoughts than your thoughts.

Memory Verse:
Psalm 147:5 Great is our Lord and mighty in power; His understanding has no limit.

For Further Reading:
The Jesus Storybook Bible - "Filled full!" pg. 244
Matthew 14:14-21

 ## Talking with God

Infinite God,

Thank you that you can do anything you want. Help me to remember that you are God and I am not. Thank you for loving me without limits! Amen.

 ## Praising God

Call To Me- Jeremiah 33:3
vol 1 Seeds of Courage by Seeds Family Worship

God is...Creator

God made everything we see around us, and YOU are His most valuable creation!

The Bible tells us that God made people, animals, plants, the ocean, the sky, the earth, the sun... whew! From nothing, He created everything that we see around us. He made the tiniest cells in our bodies and the giant planets swirling in the sky. He is an amazing creator, and YOU are the creation He is most proud of.

What art projects have you made recently at school or with your family? You might have used paint, glue, glitter, scissors, and colored paper to make a beautiful piece of art. Once you decided it was just the way you wanted it, you may have hung it on the refrigerator for everyone to see how good it was. I bet you were proud of your work and really liked it. You were the maker of that art.

You might be able to make a fantastic art project, but did you make your own body? Did you make your arms, feet, and nose? No, you did not make yourself. So who did?

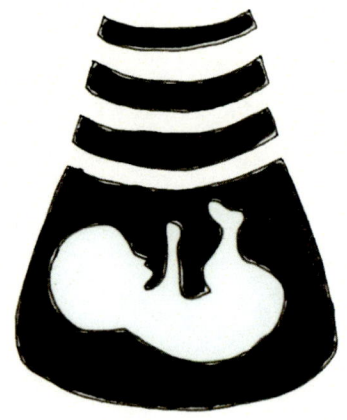

Have you ever seen an ultra-sound picture of yourself before you were born? Most of them are fuzzy, black and white pictures with a big blob in the middle. But, if you look closely, you might be able to see the shape of an arm, a foot, or a nose. We all started as tiny babies inside our mother's belly. God took a little bit of your mom and a little bit of your dad, mixed it together and created a very special YOU.

God made you just the way He wants you to be. He gave all of us the important job of taking care of the world He created.

You are Wonderfully Made

God made you exactly the way He wants you to be. You were born because God wants you to exist, and He has special plans for your life. In many ways, you are made like God so that you can show His character to others.

Spending Time With God

Listening to God

Isaiah 44:24 This is what the LORD says— your Redeemer, who formed you in the womb: I am the LORD, the Maker of all things, who stretches out the heavens, who spreads out the earth by myself.

Genesis 5:1-2 When God created mankind, He made them in the likeness of God. He created them male and female and blessed them.

Memory Verse:
Genesis 1:1 In the beginning, God created the heavens and the earth.

For Further Reading:
The Jesus Storybook Bible - "The beginning: a perfect home" pg. 18
Genesis 1-2

Talking with God

Creator God,

Thank you for making me just the way you want me to be. Help me to remember that you are proud of me and made me to be a very special part of your creation. Thank you for making all the animals and plants on Earth. Help me to take care of the world you've created. Amen.

Praising God

God is Creator - Genesis 1:1-3
vol 7 The Character of God by Seeds Family Worship

Wonderfully Made - Psalm 139:14
vol 5 The Power of Encouragement by Seeds Family Worship

God is...Eternal
God has no beginning and no end. He is forever.

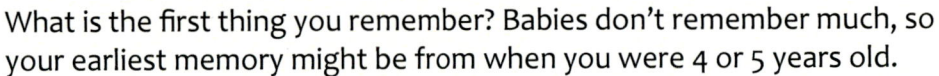

What is the first thing you remember? Babies don't remember much, so your earliest memory might be from when you were 4 or 5 years old. Ask the person reading this book about their earliest memory. They might have to think waaaaay back to when they were little.

You might not remember when you were born, but your mom definitely remembers that day. You were loved from the beginning, and even though you don't remember it, your family probably has pictures of that big day!

God is different. He is uncreated or self-existent, meaning He did not have a beginning. Did you also know that God has no end? He always was and always will be. He is eternal. That means He is forever and ever, and ever, and ever… and all the evers you can think of.

Have you ever been to a parade or seen one on TV? Marching bands, giant balloons, and people tossing candy walk down the street waving at the crowds. In cities, some people might watch a parade from the top of tall buildings to get the best view.

Imagine you are in the marching band. Which instrument would you want to play? If you were marching in the parade, you couldn't see the front of the parade or the back of the parade. You could only see the people right next to you. Now imagine you are one of the people watching the parade from the top of a tall building. From up high, you can see the entire parade - front, middle, and back!

We are like the person in the marching band, only able to see what is happening right around us. But God is like the person watching the parade from up high. He is above "time" and can see the beginning, middle, and end. God has the best view, so we can trust He knows what happens next!

You have Eternal Life
Everyone who believes in Jesus will live forever with God! Our life on Earth has a beginning and an end, but our life in heaven with God has no end. We get to love God and be loved by Him forever!

Spending Time With God

 ## Listening to God

Isaiah 26:4 Trust in the LORD forever, for the LORD Himself, is the Rock eternal.

Psalm 136:1 Give thanks to the Lord, for He is good. His love endures forever.

Memory Verse:
John 3:16 For God so loved the world that He gave His only Son, that whoever believes in Him shall not perish but have eternal life. (ESV)

For Further Reading:
The Jesus Storybook Bible - "Going home" pg. 318
John 14

 ## Talking with God

Eternal God,

Sometimes it is hard to understand things. Help us to trust what you tell us about yourself. You are **eternal** so we can know you will never end. You have **always** been and **always** will be. Thank you that we can live in heaven eternally with you! Amen.

 ## Praising God

God is Everlasting - Psalm 90:1-2
vol 7 The Character of God by Seeds Family Worship

Eternal Life - John 3:16
vol 2 Seeds of Faith by Seeds Family Worship

God is...Self-Sufficient

God depends on nothing to exist. Everything depends on Him.

If you could have any type of pet, what would you choose?
Imagine that you were given a goldfish. You'd need to give it food and clean its water to keep it alive. If you stopped giving it food, that poor goldfish would stop existing. The fish needs you to live. It depends on you to exist. And do you know what? We need God to exist. Not only did He create us, but He gives us every breath we take to keep us alive. We depend on God.

God is different; He depends on nothing to exist. He is self-sufficient. Your goldfish needs food, but God doesn't need anything. In fact, before He created the Earth and people, He was all that existed. This means that God can never stop existing. He needs nothing and depends on nothing, so God will always be. He will never leave!

Sometimes we think that we can live life without God's help. The truth is, we need God for everything, big or small. Practice being God-dependent by saying, "I can do all things through God who gives me strength!"

You are God-Dependent

You need God. He gives you every breath you take and is with you for every step you take. Depend on God to care for you and lead you where He wants you to go.

Spending Time With God

 ## Listening to God

Acts 17:24-25 The God who made the world and everything in it is the Lord of heaven and earth and does not live in temples built by human hands. And He is not served by human hands, as if He needed anything. Rather, He Himself gives everyone life and breath and everything else.

Colossians 1:17 He is before all things, and in Him all things hold together. (ESV)

Memory Verse:
Philippians 4:13 I can do all things through Him who strengthens me. (ESV)

For Further Reading:
The Jesus Storybook Bible - "God makes a way" pg. 92
Exodus 14-15

 ## Talking with God

Self-Sufficient God,

Thank you that you don't need anything to exist. Thank you that you will never leave. Please help me to remember that you will always be there. Help me to depend on you for everything big and small. Amen.

 ## Praising God

The Secret - Philippians 4:12-13
vol 5 The Power of Encouragement by Seeds Family Worship

Life And Breath - Acts 17:24-25
vol 4 Seeds of Purpose by Seeds Family Worship

God is...Omniscient

God knows everything about everything. He is all-knowing and doesn't need to learn.

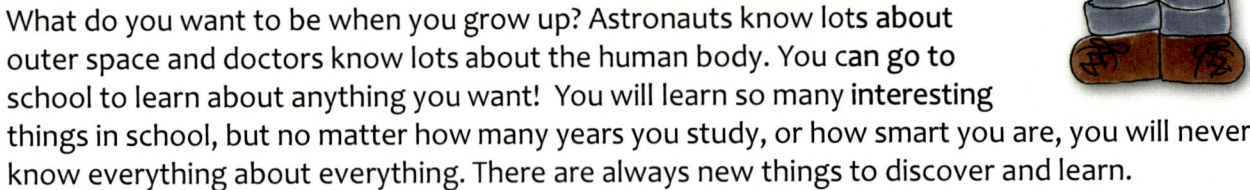

What do you want to be when you grow up? Astronauts know lots about outer space and doctors know lots about the human body. You can go to school to learn about anything you want! You will learn so many interesting things in school, but no matter how many years you study, or how smart you are, you will never know everything about everything. There are always new things to discover and learn.

God is different. He already knows everything about everything. He is omniscient, or all-knowing. He doesn't need to go to school or to learn. God knows everything about YOU: who you are, what you do, and what you need.

God knows who you are:
Does the president of the United States know your name? Probably not. But the God of the entire world does. He knows your name, your birthday, your favorite flavor of ice cream, and what you did at school today. God knows what you think and the number of hairs on your head.

God knows what you do:
God knows when you share half of your cracker with your little brother, and He knows when you sneak a cookie before dinner. You can never hide from God. He knows all the good things you do and all the bad things (called sin). God doesn't like it when you sin, and God wants you to tell Him your sins (called confession) so He can forgive and heal your heart. But do you know what? God loves you even when you sin. In fact, He knew you were going to sin before you did it.

God knows what you need:
God knows when you fall down and scrape your knee. He knows when you feel nervous to play at your piano recital. He knows when you feel alone on the playground and need a friend. God cares about the things that happen in your life, and you can always ask God to help you!

You are Known

God knows who you are, what you do, and what you need! You are deeply and completely known by God.

18

Spending Time With God

 ## Listening to God

Psalm 139:1-5 You have searched me, LORD, and you know me.
You know when I sit and when I rise; you perceive my thoughts from afar.
You discern my going out and my lying down; you are familiar with all my ways.
Before a word is on my tongue you, LORD, know it completely.

Memory Verse:
Matthew 6:31-32 Do not worry, saying, 'What shall we eat?' or 'What shall we drink?' or 'What shall we wear?' Your heavenly Father knows that you need them.

For Further Reading:
The Jesus Storybook Bible - "The Singer" pg. 228
Matthew 6:25-34

 ## Talking with God

Omniscient God,

You know everything! Thank you for knowing about everything so I don't have to. I can trust you to take care of me. Thank you that you know me completely and that you love me when I do good things and when I make bad choices. Thank you for knowing how I feel and what I need. Amen.

 ## Praising God

Seek First - Matthew 6:31-34
vol 4 Seeds of Purpose by Seeds Family Worship

God is...Omnipotent

God is all-powerful. There are no limits to God's power, and nothing is too hard for Him to do.

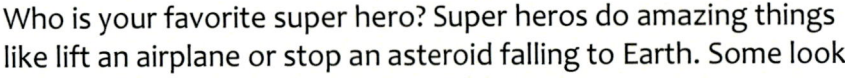

Who is your favorite super hero? Super heros do amazing things like lift an airplane or stop an asteroid falling to Earth. Some look like regular people who turn out to have incredible super powers...ta-da! Have you ever seen the World's Strongest Man competitions on TV? Big guys with lots of muscles carry giant logs or pull huge trucks with their bodies. It's fun to watch them show off their strength.

God is stronger than the world's strongest man, and He is stronger than all the super heros put together. God is omnipotent, or all-powerful. There are no limits to God's power and nothing is too hard for Him to do. As people our muscles get tired, and we are limited by the laws of nature that God has put in place on Earth. But God is outside of our world, and He can do anything He decides to do. He is supernatural and almighty.

One of the biggest examples of God's power is His power over death. Sometimes doctors are able to help sick people get better, but eventually everyone dies. People have no power to stop death. But Jesus, who is God the Son, has the power to stop death. In the ultimate act of power, Jesus brought Himself back to life after He was put to death on a cross. Jesus showed us that God has power over everything, including life and death.

In your life, you may face things that seem too hard or too big for you to handle. Maybe your family goes through a hard time or a kid at school is unkind to you at recess. Maybe you have trouble sitting still in class or remembering your spelling words. You don't have to face problems alone! God, the almighty, all-powerful, omnipotent One, knows what you need and wants to help you. He knows you are weak compared to Him, and He wants to give you His strength. Just ask Him and He'll be there with all His power to rescue you. He is the ultimate super hero!

You are Rescued

God has rescued you from sin and death. God gives you His strength when you are weak. Just ask God to rescue you and He will!

Spending Time With God

 ## Listening to God

Job 42:2 I know that you can do anything, and no one can stop you. (NLT)

1 Corinthians 2:5 That your faith might not rest on human wisdom, but on God's power.

Memory Verse:
Psalm 46:1 God is our refuge and strength, an ever-present help in trouble.

For Further Reading:
The Jesus Storybook Bible - "The Captain of the storm" pg. 236
Matthew 8:23-27

 ## Talking with God

Omnipotent God,

Thank you for being strong when I am not. You are all-powerful and can do anything you decide to do. You even have power over death, wow! Help me to remember that I can ask you for help when I face hard things. Amen.

 ## Praising God

Refuge And Strength- Psalm 46:1-2
vol 1 Seeds of Courage by Seeds Family Worship

God is...Omnipresent
God is everywhere all the time.

Have you ever wished to be in two places at once? What if you were invited to a birthday party AND to the zoo with Grandma on the same day? It would be nice if you could split yourself into two people and go to both at the same time! But there is only one of you.

God is different. All of Him is everywhere all the time. He is omnipresent. The word *present* means near, and *omni* means all or every. So omnipresent means that God is always near to everyone. It's hard to imagine, isn't it!

There are over 7 billion people in the world. That's a lot of zeros and a lot of people!

7,000,000,000

How can God be near to every single person at the same time? God is above and outside of time and our physical world. He can see everyone and everything all the time. He can see the kids in Asia, in Europe, in Africa, in South America, and the kids in the United States. He is with you when you are at school and when you are at home. God is not a force or an energy floating around in the air. He's not in the trees and rocks. He is a personal God who wants to be near to every person because He loves us so much.

Think of your best friend or your siblings. Why do you run to your friend on the playground or invite your brother to play a board game? When Daddy comes home from work, why do you run to the door and jump on him? You love them, and you want to be near to them. That's how much God loves you. He wants to be near you all the time! So run to your Father God, and you will never be alone.

You are Never Alone
God is always near to you, so you are never alone! You can talk to God any time you want by praying, and He always hears you.

Spending Time With God

 ## Listening to God

Proverbs 15:3 The eyes of the LORD are everywhere, keeping watch on the wicked and the good.

Hebrews 13:5b God has said, "Never will I leave you; never will I forsake you."

Memory Verse:
Isaiah 41:10 So do not fear, for I am with you; do not be dismayed, for I am your God. I will strengthen you and help you; I will uphold you with my righteous right hand.

For Further Reading:
The Jesus Storybook Bible - "The warrior leader" pg. 108
Joshua 3 and 6

 ## Talking with God

Omnipresent God,

Thank you for wanting to be near to me and for never leaving me. Help me to never hide from you, even when I make mistakes. Help me to always want to be near to you too! Amen.

 ## Praising God

Do Not Fear - Isaiah 41:10
vol 1 Seeds of Courage by Seeds Family Worship

Mighty To Save - Zephaniah 3:17
vol 3 Seeds of Praise by Seeds Family Worship

God is...Sovereign

God is in control of us and the whole world. He knows what is best for our lives!

Who are the sources of authority in your life? Who is in charge of you? You might think of your parents, your teachers, the police, your Sunday school teacher, or the bus driver. As a kid, lots of people are in charge of you because you are learning to make good choices. The adults in your life are there to help you learn what is right and wrong.

Someday, a LONG time from now, you will become an adult. When you are an adult the list of people in charge gets smaller. Maybe just the police and your boss at work. But there's one source of authority who is above all the others and will always be first in charge. He is above you, your parents, your teacher, the police, and even the president! You guessed it… God is the one in charge of everyone. He is sovereign over, or completely in charge of, His creation. If you think about it, God is the best person to be in charge; He sees everything, He knows everything, He has all the power, and He will never end. He is the best person for the job of running the world.

Do you sometimes find it hard to submit to the authority in your life? Sometimes it's hard to clean up your room when your mom asks you to. Sometimes it's hard to keep all four legs of the chair on the ground when your teacher tells you to.

Submitting to the adults in charge of you helps you practice submitting to God. God has put adults in your life to teach you what to do and how to obey so that when you become an adult you will submit your life choices to God's sovereign control.

You are Taken Care Of

You are taken care of by God who controls the whole world. You submit to God's authority by obeying Him and the adults that take care of you. You are not in control of your life, the God who loves you is!

Spending Time With God

Listening to God

2 Samuel 7:22a How great you are, Sovereign LORD! There is no one like you, and there is no God but you.

Colossians 3:20 Children, obey your parents in everything, for this pleases the Lord.

Memory Verse:
Philippians 2:10-11 At the name of Jesus every knee should bow, in heaven and on earth and under the earth, and every tongue acknowledge that Jesus Christ is Lord, to the glory of God the Father.

For Further Reading:
The Jesus Storybook Bible - "The forgiving prince" pg. 76
Genesis 37, 40-41

Talking with God

Sovereign God,

I am thankful that you are in charge because you know best. Help me to learn to obey the adults in charge of me so that I can learn to make good choices and submit my life to you. Amen.

Praising God

Jesus Christ Is Lord- Philippians 2:9-11
vol 8 The Word of God by Seeds Family Worship

*Be Still-*Psalm 46:10
vol 3 Seeds of Praise by Seeds Family Worship

God is...Trinity

God is one God in three persons: Father, Son, and Holy Spirit. They are the same in attributes but different in roles.

Have you ever seen a picture of a pyramid in Egypt? A long time ago the Egyptians believed in many gods: the sun god, the river god, the sky god. They didn't know about the one true God until Abraham's descendent Joseph told them, and then his descendent Moses showed them the true God's power. The Bible says very clearly that there is only one true God, not many made-up gods like the Egyptians thought.

The Bible also talks about God in three persons: God the Father, God the Son, and God the Holy Spirit. But wait...how can there be one God but also three? The trinity is one of the attributes of God that our minds can't fully understand. But we can trust that the all-knowing (omniscient) God has everything under control (sovereign) even when our small minds don't completely understand.

What are your jobs around the house? Maybe you help with the dishes, feed the dog, or take out the trash. The Father, Son, and Holy Spirit have the same attributes equally, but they have different jobs. God the Father made us, God the Son (Jesus) died on the cross to save us, and the Holy Spirit lives in the hearts of Christians to help us.

So when someone says "the Father," think *God who made me*. When someone says "Jesus," think *God who saves me*. When someone says "Holy Spirit," think *God who helps me*. The Father, Son, and Holy Spirit make up the one true God we call the Trinity.

There are three persons in the one true and living God: the Father, the Son (Jesus), and the Holy Spirit. They are the same in substance, equal in power and glory. – New City Catechism

You have a Helper

When you believe in God, He gives you a special helper to live in you, the Holy Spirit. The Spirit helps you understand truth, reminds you what is right and wrong, and makes you brave to tell others who God is.

Spending Time With God

 ## Listening to God

Acts 1:8 [Jesus said,] "But you will receive power when the Holy Spirit has come upon you, and you will be my witnesses in Jerusalem and in all Judea and Samaria, and to the end of the earth." (ESV)

1 Corinthians 3:16 You are God's temple and God's Spirit lives in you. (ESV)

Memory Verse:
Matthew 28:19 Go therefore and make disciples of all nations, baptizing them in the name of the Father and of the Son and of the Holy Spirit.

For Further Reading:
The Jesus Storybook Bible - "Heaven breaks through" pg. 200
Matthew 3

 ## Talking with God

Father in heaven,

Thank you for creating me, for saving me through Jesus's death on the cross, and for sending the Holy Spirit to help me.
Amen.

Go - Matthew 28:19
vol 5 The Power of Encouragement by Seeds Family Worship

God's UNIQUE Attributes

God is   You are

Unchanging  **Secure**
always the same   *always loved by God*

Infinite  **Loved Without Limits**
without limits   *finite but infinitely loved*

Creator  **Wonderfully Made**
maker of everything   *made in God's image*

Eternal  **Have Eternal Life**
no beginning or end   *loved by God forever*

Self-Sufficient  **God-Dependent**
depends on nothing   *in need of God*

Omniscient  **Known**
knows everything   *deeply known by God*

Omnipotent  **Rescued**
all-powerful   *given God's strength*

Omnipresent  **Never Alone**
everywhere all the time   *always heard by God*

Sovereign  **Taken Care Of**
in control of the world   *not in control*

Trinity  **Have a Helper**
Father, Son, & Holy Spirit   *sent with God's help*

Let's Review!

Memorizing God's Word

Hebrews 13:8 Jesus Christ is the same yesterday and today and forever.

Psalm 147:5 Great is our Lord and mighty in power; His understanding has no limit.

Genesis 1:1 In the beginning, God created the heavens and the earth.

John 3:16 For God so loved the world that He gave His only Son, that whoever believes in Him shall not perish but have eternal life. (ESV)

Philippians 4:13 I can do all things through Him who strengthens me. (ESV)

Matthew 6:31-32 Do not worry, saying, 'What shall we eat?' or 'What shall we drink?' or 'What shall we wear?' Your heavenly Father knows that you need them.

Psalm 46:1 God is our refuge and strength, an ever-present help in trouble.

Isaiah 41:10 So do not fear, for I am with you; do not be dismayed, for I am your God. I will strengthen you and help you; I will uphold you with my righteous right hand.

Philippians 2:10-11 At the name of Jesus every knee should bow, in heaven and on earth and under the earth, and every tongue acknowledge that Jesus Christ is Lord, to the glory of God the Father.

Matthew 28:19 Go therefore and make disciples of all nations, baptizing them in the name of the Father and of the Son and of the Holy Spirit.

God's UNIQUE Attributes
Can you name them all?

30

Quiz Time!

Section 2
God's MORAL Attributes

In the next few chapters we'll learn about the moral attributes of God. Remember, attributes are characteristics that describe what we are like. These next attributes describe what God is like in His relationship to us. With the Holy Spirit's help, we can and should imitate many of them.

What Does Imitate Mean?
To imitate is to follow, copy, or be like someone else. If you could pick someone to imitate, who would it be? You might laugh just like your mom or play soccer like your brother. Have you ever read a book or watched a movie about a famous person? You might want to imitate those people as you grow up. We all need people to look up to and inspire us!

The best person to imitate is God, and He has given us the ability to copy some of His attributes. While we can never be perfect like God is, the Holy Spirit can help us become more and more like Him. When people watch how Christians act, they should get a better idea of what God is like. That is our important job, showing the world who God is!

Ephesians 5:1
Therefore be imitators of God, as beloved children... (ESV)

1 Timothy 4:12
Don't let anyone look down on you because you are young, but set an example for the believers in speech, in conduct, in love, in faith and in purity.

Moral Attributes

- faithful
- good
- just
- righteous
- merciful
- gracious
- loving
- holy
- jealous
- wise
- truthful

We can never know who or what we are till we know at least something of what God is.
-A.W. Tozer

God is...Good

God is the standard to determine what is good and what is not. God's ultimate goodness was shown through Jesus's life and death on the cross.

How can we know what is good and what is bad? By getting to know God we learn how to love good things. God is good, but people are not. We are born sinful. No matter how hard we **try we can never** be as good as God.

The moon is 238,855 miles from Earth. If you could drive a car to the moon it would take you almost 6 months to get there. That's really really really far away! Now imagine that your baby brother tried to reach the moon by jumping. He wouldn't reach very high. Imagine that you jumped. You'd reach a little higher. If your dad jumped, he'd reach even farther, and if a basketball player jumped, he'd reach even farther still. Did anyone reach the moon? Not the baby, not you, not your dad, and not even the super tall basketball player. It is SO far away that no one, no matter how tall or how strong, can ever jump to the moon.

Just like no one can jump to the moon, no one can ever be as good as God. No matter how hard you try or how many good choices you make, you will never be good enough to meet God's perfect standard. That's why God came to Earth as a man, Jesus. Jesus lived a perfect life and met God's standard of goodness. When we accept Jesus's goodness instead of trying to be good on our own, God rescues us from our sinful life. God gives us two good gifts: freedom from sin and eternal life with Him.

You are Not Good Enough

You will often make wrong choices, and you can never be as good as God. But Jesus meets God's perfect standard and offers to exchange your sin for His goodness when you trust Him with your life.

Spending Time With God

📖 Listening to God

Psalm 119:68 You are good, and what you do is good; teach me your decrees.

Romans 12:9 Hate what is evil; cling to what is good.

Philippians 4:8 Finally, brothers and sisters, whatever is true, whatever is noble, whatever is right, whatever is pure, whatever is lovely, whatever is admirable—if anything is excellent or praiseworthy—think about such things.

Memory Verse:
Psalm 107:1 Give thanks to the LORD, for He is good; His love endures forever.

For Further Reading:
The Jesus Storybook Bible - "Ten ways to be perfect" pg. 100 Exodus 20:1-17, 32:1-9
The Jesus Storybook Bible - "Washed with tears" pg. 280 Luke 7:36-50

🙏 Talking with God

Good God,

Thank you that you are perfectly good so that I don't have to be perfect. Thank you for giving us your goodness through Jesus. Amen.

🎵 Praising God

The Good Song - Psalm 34:10
vol 1 Seeds of Courage by Seeds Family Worship

God is...Just

Everything God does is right and fair. When we sin and go against God's commands, He is right to punish us as we deserve.

God is a just God, which means that everything He does is right and fair. He determines what people should do, and He holds people to that standard equally.

In our country there are laws made by the government. If a grown-up is pulled over by a police officer for driving too fast, then they broke the law and must pay the fine as punishment. Have you ever broken a rule at your house? If you break a rule, it is just for you to get punished; maybe you sit in time-out or have a privilege taken away.

God's rules are the most important ones to follow. God is always right, always fair, and always just. We should imitate God by loving what is right and hating what is wrong.

God's hatred of bad things is called wrath. Wrath might be a new word to you; it is similar to anger. Have you ever been angry? We all get frustrated or angry sometimes. God's wrath is different than our anger because His wrath is not out of control or mean. He is angry because of sin and injustice. When people sin against God and reject His love, God is right to be angry. He doesn't want us to be separated from Him or to be hurt by doing bad things.

Adam and Eve disobeyed God by believing Satan's lies, wanting to be in control, and doing something God said not to. As a result, they had to leave the garden where they lived in a close relationship with God. We are just like they were. We have sinned and deserve to be separated from God's presence and love forever. We all deserve God's wrath because of our sin.

Thankfully, Jesus satisfied God's wrath by taking our punishment and dying on the cross. His death fulfilled God's just hatred of our sin so that we are no longer separated from God.

You are a Sinner

You have sinned and acted in ways that go against God's commands. It would be just for you to be separated from the holy, good God forever.

Spending Time With God

Listening to God

Psalm 11:7 For the LORD is righteous, He loves justice; the upright will see His face.

Romans 1:18 The wrath of God is being revealed from heaven against all the godlessness and wickedness of people, who suppress the truth by their wickedness.

Numbers 14:18a The LORD is slow to anger, abounding in love and forgiving sin. Yet He does not leave the guilty unpunished.

Memory Verse:
Romans 3:23 For all have sinned and fall short of the glory of God.

For Further Reading:
The Jesus Storybook Bible - "A new beginning" pg. 38
Genesis 6:11-14, 7-9

Talking with God

Just God,

You are always fair and decide what is right and wrong. Help me to love what is right and hate what is wrong. You are right to be angry about the bad things people do. I'm sorry that I have sinned and deserve to be separated from you. Thank you that Jesus took my punishment so I can be in your family. Amen.

Praising God

The Wages And The Gift- Romans 3:23 & 6:23
vol 6 Seeds of Character by Seeds Family Worship

God is...Righteous

God is completely without sin.

[Parent note: You will need 2 plain white pieces of paper, 1 crayon, and stickers]

When was the last time you sinned by doing something wrong? Most of us probably did something wrong today. We are born with a sin nature, and the Bible says that all people have sinned. God, though, is completely and totally sinless, or righteous. He has never ever sinned.

Look at this blank piece of white paper. It's perfectly clean and "without sin." Now when I draw a tiny dot on the paper, is it perfectly clean anymore? Nope. The wrong things we do like lie to your mom or think a mean thought about a friend, are like dots on the paper. Whether you have lots of dots, one giant dot, or just a few medium dots, your paper is not perfectly clean; it's not righteous. No one in all of time has ever lived a perfect and righteous life… except Jesus.

Do any of your friends or family live far away in another state or country? It's hard to be separated from people we love. The Bible tells us that our sins separate us from God. Sinful, unrighteous people can't be in the presence of a sinless, righteous God. God does not want to be separated from us, the people He loves! But since we all sin, how can we possibly become righteous? How can we be in a close relationship with God?

Some people try to be righteous by doing more good things than bad things. Let's call these stickers "good things," like sharing with your brother and obeying your parents. It's wonderful when you do good things! If I add lots of good stickers to the paper I may be able to cover up some dots of sin. But are the sin dots gone? Is the paper perfectly clean? Nope! No matter how many good things you do, it will never erase your sin. You can never be righteous, even if you do lots of good things.

So if we can never do enough good things to be righteous, how can we fix our separation from God? The good news is that Jesus never sinned. He was the only one who lived a perfect life. His life looks like this other perfectly clean sheet of paper. No sin dots at all!

When Jesus died on the cross, He took our piece of paper with sin dots and wrote His name on the top. When I write "Jesus" at the top of your paper it shows that all your sins belong to Him. Then Jesus gave you His perfectly clean sheet of paper. When I write your name at the top of the clean paper it shows that Jesus traded with you. You have Jesus's righteousness and can be near to God! All you need to do is accept Jesus's perfect piece of paper as yours.

You are Right With God

You have sinned, separating you from God. But Jesus gives you His righteous life so you can have a relationship God!

Spending Time With God

Listening to God

Isaiah 59:2 But your [sins] have separated you from your God; your sins have hidden His face from you, so that He will not hear.

Ephesians 2:13 But now in Christ Jesus you who once were far away have been brought near by the blood of Christ.

Memory Verse:
Romans 5:8 But God demonstrates His own love for us in this: While we were still sinners, Christ died for us.

For Further Reading:
The Jesus Storybook Bible - "The sun stops shining" pg. 302
The Jesus Storybook Bible - "God's wonderful surprise" pg. 310
Matthew 27-28

Talking with God

Righteous God,

I have sinned many times, but you are completely without sin. Thank you that Jesus traded my sinful life with His righteous life so that I can be in a close relationship with you! I accept the gift of His righteous life. Amen.

Praising God

Hey Man- Romans 5:8, 6:23
vol 2 Seeds of Faith by Seeds Family Worship

God is...Merciful

Mercy is forgiveness toward someone who deserves punishment. God has forgiven us even though we are sinners who deserve separation from God.

Imagine that your mom trusted you with a box of crayons and told you to only draw on paper. What if you decided to draw on the walls instead? Yikes! You might feel ashamed of doing a bad thing and hide in your closet away from your mom. How would your mom react when she saw your crayon-covered walls? She would not be happy that you disobeyed, and she probably wouldn't trust you with crayons again for a while. Your mom is right to be angry about your wrong action, and she would be just to punish you as you deserve.

Sin hurts our relationship with God. When we sin we want to hide from God just like Adam and Eve did in the garden of Eden. Sin causes separation and hurt. Imagine that you felt guilty and were hiding from your mom, but because your mom loves you SO much she forgives you and tells you that you won't be punished. That's mercy. You deserve to be in trouble, but instead you are forgiven! Instead of hiding, you'd feel thankful and give your mom a big hug. Forgiveness leads to nearness and healing.

Because God has forgiven us for all our sins and exchanged our sinful life (paper of black dots) with Jesus's life (the perfectly clean paper), we can be close to God. Our guilty hearts can be healed! When you sin, don't hide from God, run to Him. Confess your sins to God, who already knows, and tell Him you are sorry. He will always forgive you, heal your heart, and bring you near to Him.

Just as God has forgiven us, we should forgive others when they do something wrong. If a friend at school laughs when you fall down but later says they are sorry, what should you do? You can choose to stay angry and not forgive that friend, or you can choose to be like God and forgive your friend. Your friendship can be healed and you can play together again. Forgive others just like God has forgiven you.

You are Forgiven

When you tell God you are sorry for your sins, He always forgives you. Your sin no longer separates you from Him and your heart can be healed. You should forgive people that hurt you just like God has forgiven you!

Spending Time With God

📖 Listening to God

Ephesians 2:4-5 Because of His great love for us, God, who is rich in mercy, made us alive with Christ even when we were dead in [sin].

Ephesians 4:32 Be kind and compassionate to one another, forgiving each other, just as in Christ God forgave you.

Memory Verse:
1 John 1:9 If we confess our sins, He is faithful and just and will forgive us our sins and purify us from all unrighteousness.

For Further Reading:
The Jesus Storybook Bible - "Running away" pg. 272
Luke 15

🙏 Talking with God

Merciful God,

Thank you that you have forgiven me of my sins and that you will always forgive me when I ask. Help me to never hide from you, but to run to you for forgiveness. Help me to forgive other people the same way you have forgiven me. Amen.

🎵 Praising God

The Character Song- Romans 5:1-5
vol 6 Seeds of Character by Seeds Family Worship

God is...Gracious

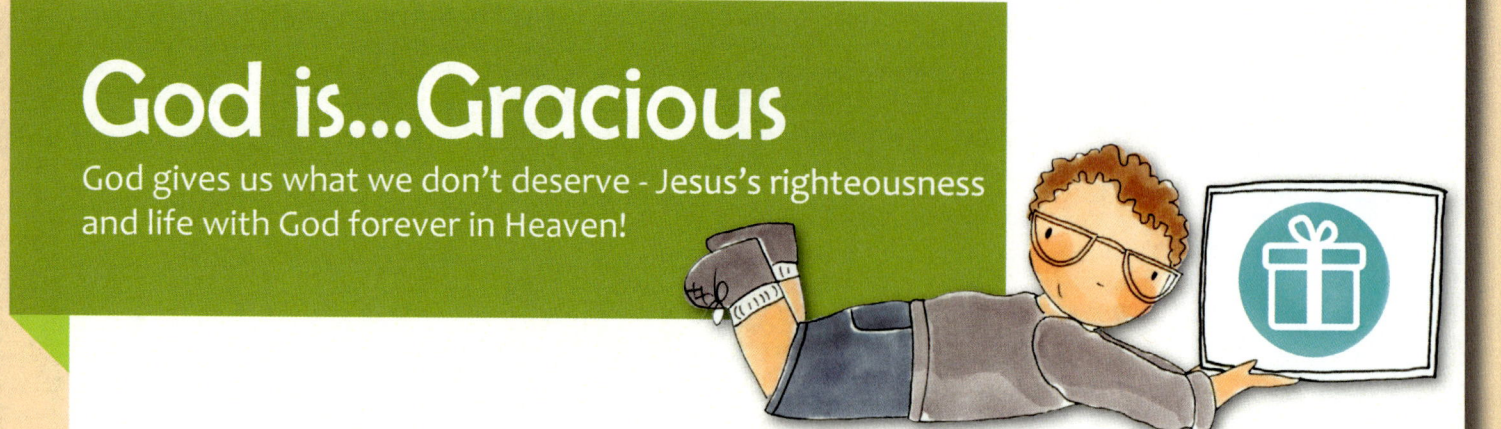

God gives us what we don't deserve - Jesus's righteousness and life with God forever in Heaven!

Have you ever received a special present that you did not expect? Maybe your mom surprised you with your favorite candy eventhough you didn't do anything to earn it. Or maybe your teacher gave your whole class an extra recess without earning it. Those undeserved gifts are examples of graced. Grace is receiving something good that you don't deserve.

We tend to think of ourselves as pretty good people. It's easy to be prideful and think that you are better than other kids. The truth is, we are all sinners. We all have sin dots on our paper. No one has a clean piece of paper on their own.

The grace of God is shown when He gives us Jesus's righteous life in exchange for our sinful lives. We do not deserve Jesus's righteousness, and we do not deserve to be near to God. We deserve to keep our sinful life, and we deserve to be separated from God forever. Instead, God gave us the best gift you could ever imagine. It's better than all the video games in the world and better than a new bike or a fancy dress. God gave us Jesus's righteousness so that we can be friends with God and live forever with Him.

Think about a favorite gift that you've been given. Let's say it was something you really wanted for your birthday. When you went to school, you probably told everyone about how excited you were about your cool new toy!

God's gift is bigger and more special than a new toy. Your toy will break, but God's gift of righteousness is forever. We should be excited to tell all our friends that Jesus wants to trade papers with them too!

You are Accepted

Because of God's gracious gift, you are saved from your sins and accepted by God. You can tell all your friends about God's free gift!

Spending Time With God

📖 Listening to God

Ephesians 2:8-9 For it is by grace you have been saved, through faith—and this is not from yourselves, it is the gift of God—not by works, so that no one can boast.

Acts 20: 24b My only aim is to...complete the task the Lord Jesus has given me—the task of telling others the good news of God's grace.

Memory Verse:
Romans 6:23 For the wages of sin is death, but the free gift of God is eternal life in Christ Jesus our Lord.

For Further Reading:
The Jesus Storybook Bible - "The man who didn't have any friends (none)" pg. 264
The Jesus Storybook Bible - "A new way to see" pg. 334
Luke 19:1-10 Acts 9:1-22

🙏 Talking with God

Gracious God,

Thank you for giving me what I don't deserve - the gift of Jesus's righteousness and eternal life with you in heaven! Please help me to tell my friends that they can have this gift too! Amen.

🎵 Praising God

The Wages And The Gift- Romans 3:23 & 6:23
vol 6 Seeds of Character by Seeds Family Worship

Grace (LA-DE-DA)- Ephesians 2:8
vol 2 Seeds of Faith by Seeds Family Worship

God is...Loving

God loves you because you belong to Him, not because of anything you do.

Who loves you? Most of the people that love you are in your family, including pets! Do you know why they love you? It's not because you are good at reading or a fast runner. It's not because you have pretty hair or big brown eyes. It's not because you get good grades or clean your room. You are loved because you are in your family. That's it. Whether you were born in or adopted in, your family loves you because you belong to them.

God also loves you because you belong to Him. That's it. Not because you do good things or work hard. You can't do anything to earn God's love or make Him love you more. He already loves you more than you could ever understand. You are loved by God because you are in His family. You do not have to be afraid that your mistakes make you unlovable or that God's love will leave. As a part of God's family, nothing can separate you from God's love. You are loved just as you are. When people in your life don't love you well, God always does.

What makes you feel loved? You might feel loved when someone says "I love you," gives you a hug, or spends time playing with you. Sometimes someone in your family may give you a gift to show you their love. God showed us how much He loved us when He died on the cross. Jesus gave up His life so that we could have life. Jesus was separated from God so we could be near to God. Jesus took our unrighteous paper with sinful dots so we could have a righteous paper that's perfectly clean. He made you special, He forgives you when you sin, and He wants you to accept His gift of love.

How do you show your parents that you love them? You might follow their rules, spend time with them, and give them gifts that you make. How should you show God that you love Him? Show your love for God by obeying His commands (in the Bible), by talking with Him (praying), and by loving other people. God wants to you love Him by loving others!

You are Loved

You can't earn God's love, just accept it! You should love other people the way God loves you, by putting others first.

Spending Time With God

📖 Listening to God

1 John 3:16a This is how we know what love is: Jesus Christ laid down His life for us.

Romans 8:38-39 For I am convinced that neither death nor life, neither angels nor demons, neither the present nor the future, nor any powers, neither height nor depth, nor anything else in all creation, will be able to separate us from the love of God that is in Christ Jesus our Lord.

Memory Verse:
Mark 12:30-31 'Love the Lord your God with all your heart and with all your soul and with all your mind and with all your strength.' The second is this: 'Love your neighbor as yourself.' There is no commandment greater than these.

For Further Reading:
The Jesus Storybook Bible - "A friend of little children" pg. 256
Mark 10:13-16

🙏 Talking with God

Loving God,

Thank you for loving me just because I belong to you. Help me to show my love for you by obeying your commands, spending time with you, and loving other people. Amen.

🎵 Praising God

Greatest Commandment- Mark 12:30-31
vol 4 Seeds of Purpose by Seeds Family Worship

God Is Love- 1 John 4:16
vol 7 The Character of God by Seeds Family Worship

God is...Holy

To be holy means to be set apart as special. Of all the special things, God is the most holy.

The Bible calls God holy many times. To be holy does not mean God is full of holes like Swiss cheese! To be holy means to be set apart as special. Something that is holy is unlike all other things. It is different from the others and specifically set apart to be important.

What things are special to you? I bet your birthday is a special day for you! Your birthday is set aside as a special day to celebrate your life. God has set aside special days for us to celebrate Him too, like Easter, Christmas, or every Sunday when we worship God as a church.

Out of all the special things, God is most holy: His name, His presence, and His promises. He is the most important one of all. He is even more special than Christmas or your birthday!

Before Jesus came to Earth, the only people who could go near to God were priests. Once each year a priest followed careful instructions, went into a special room called the "Holy of Holies," and sacrificed a lamb. The lamb died so that God would forgive the sins of the people for one year.

Why don't we have priests that sacrifice lambs in a special room now? When Jesus died on the cross, He became the last sacrifice. Our sins are forgiven not just for one year but forever and ever! As people who follow Jesus, we are now set apart and holy. We can go to God's presence any time we want by praying.

God has adopted us as His children into His special family! Because we are adopted children of God, we are not to live like the rest of the world, doing sinful things like we used to. We are to imitate God so that other people will want to be part of His special family too!

You are Special

God has adopted us to be special children in His set-apart family! We are not to be like the world, but we should imitate God. We are to show the world who God is by the way we live.

Spending Time With God

📖 Listening to God

1 Samuel 2:2 There is no one holy like the LORD; there is no one besides you; there is no Rock like our God.

2 Timothy 1:9a He has saved us and called us to a holy life—not because of anything we have done but because of His own purpose and grace.

Memory Verse:
Leviticus 20:26 You are to be holy to me because I, the LORD, am holy and I have set you apart from the nations to be my own.

For Further Reading:
The Jesus Storybook Bible - "The present" pg. 62
Genesis 22

🙏 Talking with God

Holy God,

You are the most set-apart, important one. Thank you that I am your special child. You are special to me, too. Please help my life make other people want to be part of your family! Amen.

🎵 Praising God

God is Holy - Isaiah 6:1-3
vol 7 The Character of God by Seeds Family Worship

God is...Jealous

God is jealous for our hearts. He wants our hearts and minds to belong only to Him, the one true God.

[Parent Note: You will need a large cup, rocks or plastic blocks, and some water]

Can you think of a time you were jealous? Maybe a classmate came to school with cool new shoes you wanted or a friend got the birthday present you were wishing for. We all struggle with wanting something that someone else has. When we compare ourselves to others and are not content with what we have, we feel jealous. That type of jealousy is not good. Comparison and discontentment will cause you to be ungrateful and unhappy.

God is jealous for His name and for His people. Wait a minute! Isn't it bad to be jealous? God's righteous jealousy is to protect His relationship with people. Some people make up pretend gods. They worship fake statues or idols instead of the one true God. God is jealous for people to love and worship only Him instead of made-up gods. God wants the hearts of people to belong to Him and Him only. Accepting Jesus's righteous life in place of our own sinful life is the only way that we can be right with God.

Sometimes we create idols in our lives that keep our hearts far from God. We may not make a statue, but we fill our hearts and minds with things other than God. We make good things like school or sports more important than God, and they become our idols.

Watch as I put rocks or plastic blocks inside this cup. The cup is like your heart, and each rock is like an activity or idol. It's easy to get focused on all our activities and pretty soon our hearts and minds are full of ourselves. But is the cup really full? No, there are still holes between the rocks. Now when I take the rocks out of the cup and pour water into the cup, is the cup full? Yes! Now it is completely full. God is like the water; only He can completely fill your heart. God is jealous for your heart. He wants it to be full of Him so that you will be completely satisfied instead of worshipping selfish idols that leave your heart with holes. When we read God's Word, learn about Him in church, and pray to Him we fill our minds and hearts with God so we will never be empty!

You are Filled By God

Fill your heart and mind with the one true God instead of trying to fill your heart with made-up gods or selfish idols.

Spending Time With God

Listening to God

Exodus 20:3-5 "You shall have no other gods before me. You shall not make for yourself an image in the form of anything in heaven above or on the earth beneath or in the waters below. You shall not bow down to them or worship them; for I, the LORD your God, am a jealous God…"

John 14:6 Jesus answered, "I am the way and the truth and the life. No one comes to the Father except through me."

Memory Verse
Acts 4:12 And there is salvation in no one else, for there is no other name under heaven given among men by which we must be saved. (ESV)

For Further Reading:
The Jesus Storybook Bible - "Treasure hunt!" pg. 250
Matthew 13:44-46, Exodus 32:1-9

Talking with God

Jealous God,

Thank you for wanting my heart to belong only to you. Please show me the things I make more important than you. Help me to fill my heart and mind with you instead of myself. Amen.

Praising God

God Is Jealous- Exodus 20:3-5a
vol 7 The Character of God by Seeds Family Worship

The Life- John 14:6, 1 John 5:11-12
vol 6 Seeds of Character by Seeds Family Worship

49

God is...Wise

God knows and does what is best for His glory and our lives.

Because God is omniscient (He knows everything), good, and loving, He is also all-wise. God knows and does what is best for His glory and for our lives.

No matter how smart you get, you will never be smarter than God. One of the biggest mistakes you can make is to think that you know best or that you don't need God's wisdom to make choices. That's called pride. Every day you make choices: obey your teacher or be disrespectful, share with your sister or argue, do your homework or be lazy, eat healthy food or junk food. As sinful people we often act based on what we want: talk back, be selfish, play games instead of doing homework, eat lots of candy. But if we have filled our minds with God's truth, we can learn to act based on His wisdom. We learn to respect authority, be kind, work hard, and treat our bodies well.

God is like a shepherd who takes care of us, His sheep. We don't know where the best grass is to eat, but God does. If we follow Him and His wisdom, He will lead us to fields of green grass. But if we try to be our own shepherd, we will get lost and our feet will get stuck between rocks. When you get lost, call to your Shepherd, God, who will always come find you! He saves us from being too independent and reminds us that depending on His wisdom is best.

You are Led by The Shepherd

We can trust that God knows and does what is best. Instead of thinking that we know best, we can ask God to lead us like a good shepherd.

Spending Time With God

📖 Listening to God

Romans 11:33 Oh, the depth of the riches of the wisdom and knowledge of God! How unsearchable His judgments, and His paths beyond tracing out!

Psalm 23:1 The LORD is my shepherd; I shall not want. He makes me lie down in green pastures. He leads me beside still waters. He restores my soul. He leads me in paths of righteousness for his name's sake. (ESV)

Memory Verse:
Proverbs 3:5-7 Trust in the LORD with all your heart and lean not on your own understanding; in all your ways submit to Him, and He will make your paths straight. Do not be wise in your own eyes; fear the LORD and turn from evil.

For Further Reading:
The Jesus Storybook Bible - "The Good Shepherd" pg. 130
Psalm 23

🙏 Talking with God

Wise God,

I praise you for knowing what is best. Please help me learn to follow your wisdom instead of thinking that I know best. Amen.

🎵 Praising God

Trust In The Lord- Proverbs 3:5-6
vol 4 Seeds of Purpose by Seeds Family Worship

God Is Wise- Romans 11:33-36
vol 7 The Character of God by Seeds Family Worship

God is...Truthful
God always tells the truth and never lies.

God never lies. Whatever He says is true and whatever commands He makes are right. Satan is called the father of lies. He likes to trick people into following his lies instead of God's truths.

How can we keep ourselves from believing Satan's lies? We need to listen to God's voice. We talk to God when we pray, and we listen to God when we read the Bible. By spending time praying and reading the Bible we have conversations with God. If we fill our minds with Bible verses, when Satan tries to tell us a lie, we can replace that lie with the truth of God's words.

Let's think of some lies you might believe and then replace those lies with the truth of God.

Lie: You should do what your friend says, not what your parents say to do.
Truth: Children, obey your parents in everything, for this pleases the Lord. Colossians 3:20

Lie: The other kids are better because they have nicer things.
Truth: Keep your lives free from the love of money; be content with what you have. Hebrews 13:5

Lie: You need to wear trendy clothes or cool athletic shoes.
Truth: Your beauty should not come from outward adornment, such as elaborate hairstyles and the wearing of gold jewelry or fine clothes. Rather, it should be that of your inner self, the unfading beauty of a gentle and quiet spirit, which is of great worth in God's sight. 1 Peter 3:3-4

Lie: You need to get the best grades or win the sports tournament to be happy.
Truth: Do not store up for yourselves treasures on earth, where moths and vermin destroy, and where thieves break in and steal. But store up for yourselves treasures in heaven, where moths and vermin do not destroy, and where thieves do not break in and steal. For where your treasure is, there your heart will be also. Matthew 6:19-21

Ask God to show you what lies you believe and then look for verses that replace those lies with truth. Reject Satan's lies, and let God's truth guide your life.

You have The Truth
When Satan lies to you, replace those lies with the truth of God. You can learn God's truth by reading His words in the Bible.

Spending Time With God

📖 Listening to God

John 8:44b …there is no truth in [Satan]. When he lies, he speaks his native language, for he is a liar and the father of lies.

Romans 10:9 If you declare with your mouth, "Jesus is Lord," and believe in your heart that God raised Him from the dead, you will be saved.

Memory Verse:
Psalm 86:11 Teach me your way, O LORD, that I may walk in your truth. (ESV)

For Further Reading:
The Jesus Storybook Bible - "The terrible lie" pg. 28   Genesis 3:1-6
The Jesus Storybook Bible - "Let's go!" pg. 208   Matthew 4:1-10

🙏 Talking with God

God of Truth,

Thank you that I can know truth through your Word, the Bible. Help me to replace Satan's lies with the truth of your words. Amen.

🎵 Praising God

Undivided Heart- Psalm 86:11-13
vol 3 Seeds of Praise by Seeds Family Worship

God is...Faithful
God always keeps His promises, so we can trust Him!

God is faithful because He keeps all His promises. God never lies, so when He makes a promise it holds true and does not change.

Have you ever made a promise? You might make a pinkie promise to be best friends forever, or a promise to be home on time for dinner. A promise is a commitment to do what you say. A person who does what he or she says is a person of integrity, or a person who is faithful. If we want to be like God, we need to be faithful to our promises, too.

Have you ever kept your promise even when it was hard? Maybe you agreed to help your mom cook muffins for a school fundraiser, but then a friend invited you over to play. You want to play, but you already agreed to bake with your mom. What should you do? You should keep your promise to your mom.

Unfortunately, people are sinful and often break promises. When someone breaks their promise, it's hard to trust them the next time they promise something. That's why it's important to be a person who keeps your word, to do what you committed to do, even if it is hard.

Thankfully, God always keeps His promises, even if we don't. He is faithful when we are not. We often mess up, but God still keeps His promises to us. Here are some of those promises:

When you sin, God has promised to forgive you. 1 John 1:9
When you feel alone, God has promised to never leave you. Hebrews 13:5
When you are afraid, God gives you peace. John 14:27
When you need something, God will take care of you. Philippians 4:19
When you believe in Jesus, you are saved. Romans 10:9

You are Blessed
You don't have to wonder if God's promises will happen, they will! You are blessed by the many promises of God.

Spending Time With God

📖 Listening to God

Deuteronomy 7:9 Know therefore that the LORD your God is God; He is the faithful God, keeping His covenant of love to a thousand generations of those who love Him and keep His commandments.

Proverbs 28:20a A faithful person will be richly blessed...

Memory Verse:
Psalm 33:4 For the word of the LORD is right and true; He is faithful in all He does.

For Further Reading:
The Jesus Storybook Bible - "Son of laughter" pg. 56
Genesis 15:5-6, 17:1-9, 17:15-22, 21:1-5

🙏 Talking with God

Faithful God,

Thank you for always being faithful even when I am not. Thank you for blessing me with your promises. Please help me to trust you and to keep my promises to others. Amen.

🎵 Praising God

God Is Faithful - 1 Corinthians 1:8-9
vol 7 The Character of God by Seeds Family Worship

God's MORAL Attributes

God is	You are
Good — standard of right & wrong	**Not Good Enough** — never meet God's standard
Just — right to punish sin	**A Sinner** — deserve punishment
Righteous — completely without sin	**Right with God** — given Jesus's righteousness
Merciful — undeserved forgiveness	**Forgiven** — healed and not separated
Gracious — undeserved gift of life	**Accepted** — just as you are
Loving — with sacrificial love	**Loved** — because you are His child
Holy — the most special	**Special** — set apart in God's family
Jealous — protective of His name & your heart	**Filled by God** — not filled with self or false gods
Wise — does what is best	**Led by the Shepherd** — can follow God's ways
Truthful — never lies	**Have the Truth** — can replace lies with truth
Faithful — always keeps promises	**Blessed** — with the promises of God

Let's Review!

Memorizing God's Word

Psalm 107:1 Give thanks to the LORD, for He is good; His love endures forever.

Romans 3:23 For all have sinned and fall short of the glory of God.

Romans 5:8 But God demonstrates His own love for us in this: While we were still sinners, Christ died for us.

1 John 1:9 If we confess our sins, He is faithful and just and will forgive us our sins and purify us from all unrighteousness.

Romans 6:23 For the wages of sin is death, but the free gift of God is eternal life in Christ Jesus our Lord.

Mark 12:30-31 'Love the Lord your God with all your heart and with all your soul and with all your mind and with all your strength.' The second is this: 'Love your neighbor as yourself.' There is no commandment greater than these.

Leviticus 20:26 You are to be holy to me because I, the LORD, am holy and I have set you apart from the nations to be my own.

Acts 4:12 And there is salvation in no one else, for there is no other name under heaven given among men by which we must be saved. (ESV)

Proverbs 3:5-7 Trust in the LORD with all your heart and lean not on your own understanding; in all your ways submit to Him, and He will make your paths straight. Do not be wise in your own eyes; fear the LORD and turn from evil.

Psalm 86:11 Teach me your way, O LORD, that I may walk in your truth… (ESV)

Psalm 33:4 For the word of the LORD is right and true; He is faithful in all He does.

God's MORAL Attributes
Can you name them all?

58

Quiz Time!

Made in United States
Orlando, FL
23 June 2025